D0757793

—Weird and Wacky Science—

LOST CITIES

Joyce Goldenstern

ENSLOW PUBLISHERS, INC.

44 Fadem Road   P.O. Box 38
Box 699   Aldershot
Springfield, N.J. 07081   Hants GU12 6BP
U.S.A.   U.K.

For Nora and my former students
at Association House:
Cedric, Marisol, Carlos.

Copyright © 1996 by Joyce Goldenstern.

Library of Congress Cataloging-in-Publication Data

Goldenstern, Joyce.
   Lost cities / Joyce Goldenstern.
      p. cm. — (Weird and wacky science)
   Includes bibliographical references and index.
   ISBN 0-89490-615-1
   1. Extinct cities—Juvenile literature. 2. Archaeology—History—Juvenile literature.
   [1. Cities and towns, Ancient. 2. Archaeology—History. 3. Civilization, Ancient.]
   I. Title. II. Series.
   CC176.G65 1996©
   930.1—dc20
                                         94-47099
                                          CIP
                                          AC

Printed in the United States of America

10 9 8 7 6 5 4 3 2 1

Illustration Credits: American Geographical Society Collection, University of
Wisconsin-Milwaukee Library, pp. 23, 37; Borromeo/Art Resource, p. 28; Enslow
Publishers, Inc., pp. 8, 18, 24, 32, 40; German Information Center, p. 17; Mary
Heller, p. 26; ©J. Michael Krouskop/Tradd Street Stock, p. 10; ©Erich Lessing/Art
Resource, p. 12; Mexican Cultural and Educational Institute Chicago, p. 7; ©Frank
Pennington/Unicorn Stock Photos, p. 34; SCALA/Art Resource, pp. 30, 33;
SEF/Art Resource, p. 4; Turkish Ministry of Tourism, p. 19; VU/©Mario Caprio,
p. 38; VU/©David L. Pearson, p. 20.

Cover Illustration: Visuals Unlimited/©David L. Pearson.

Contents

This wall painting from Bonampak shows Maya warriors in a ceremonial procession.

1

THE DYED WALLS OF BONAMPAK

"The trails, not kept open, are through long stretches of swamp and over long, steep hills. A guide is necessary no matter from which direction the site is approached."[1] Karl Ruppert wrote this advice to travelers in 1955. He also warned them about provisions. "The site is lacking in practically all facilities. Water, probably of first importance, is found . . . only in the rainy season."[2] The ruins provided little shelter. Birds, deer, and wild pigs could be hunted, but the traveler should be sure to carry some food from a nearby village. Ruppert, an anthropologist from the Carnegie Institution, was describing Bonampak, a Maya ruin in Chiapas, Mexico.

In the language of the Maya, *bonampak* means "dyed walls." In 1946, the American photographer Giles Healey had found beautiful painted murals in a temple at the site. Many adventurers were eager to see these murals; Karl Ruppert led an expedition there in 1947. His mission was to investigate the site, to make maps and diagrams of the city, and to describe the sculpture, the structures, and, most importantly, the dyed walls of Bonampak.

A City Lost to Whom?

Many writers have called Bonampak a lost city, but to the Lacandón Indians who live in Chiapas, Bonampak was not a lost city at all. The Lacandón, descendants of the Maya, sometimes visited the ruins of their ancestors. From time to time, they would chop away weeds on the overgrown trails to return to this sacred spot, but even for the Lacandón, the significance of the city with its magnificent murals had been lost. More than a thousand years had passed since Maya artists painted the murals in about A.D. 800. The Lacandón spoke a different language from that of their forebears; their customs had changed. What story did the city have to tell? Not even the Lacandón could say.

Aside from the Lacandón, no one in modern times knew about Bonampak. Then, in 1946, the United Fruit Company hired Giles Healey to make a documentary film about Maya ruins. Healey hoped to film as many sites as possible.[3] For a few months, he lived among the Lacandón, hoping to gain their confidence so that they would show him unexplored sites. Several Lacandón guides agreed to lead Healey through the rain forest to Bonampak.

Preparing for Battle

His first view of Bonampak did not impress Healey. Most of the structures stood in shambles; weeds and vines grew from crumbling walls.

6

Healey began shooting photographs of sculptures and inscriptions.

The guides had more to show him: Hidden behind dense vegetation, stood a temple with three rooms. Immense murals graced the walls of each room. The grime of centuries had dulled the colors of the murals, but later, when archaeologists smeared kerosene on the walls, magnificent colors were uncovered—blue sky over battle scenes, red pigment in indoor scenes, green swirls outlined in red suggesting vegetation, and white-clothed figures.

More impressive than the color, though, were the line and form of the murals. The balanced compositions drew the viewer's eye to dramatic action scenes. The murals in each room told part of what seemed to be one entire story. In the first room, men disguised themselves as animal gods: One wore a pointed snout, another dressed as an alligator, and a third threatened others with a huge crab claw.

In another panel, women observed attendants dressing a royal chief in an elaborate jaguar skin. Twelve musicians nearby prepared for some type of ceremony in preparation for a battle. Five musicians shook rattles, one beat a drum, three struck tortoise shells with antlers, one blew a whistle, and two sounded trumpets.

A Surprise Attack

The action continued in the second room, where a raid was in progress. Painted warriors dressed in costumes and jewelry were attacking a village in what seemed to be a surprise raid. Their victims had no weapons and were easily captured by spear-wielding warriors, one of whom dragged a prisoner away by his hair.

In another part of the mural, prisoners pricked and cut their fingers and hands. What did this bloodletting signify? Some anthropologists thought it had to do with the Maya custom of leaving handprints on walls. The prisoners may have been preparing to leave their marks in blood. The Lacandón still believed in recent times that red handprints on a building were a sign of completion[4].

8

Other anthropologists wondered if the bloodletting signaled something more sinister—the forthcoming human sacrifice.

In the third room, the warriors celebrated their victory with a dance and sacrificial ceremony. Again the musicians sounded their instruments. The body of a dead enemy soldier was sprawled out on some steps. Presumably he had just been sacrificed; a captor held a vessel with human blood and a heart in it. The blood was to be smeared on an idol.[5]

What Did It Mean?

Anthropologists try to figure out what such scenes tell us about life in ancient times. Cultural anthropologists study customs, like the Maya and Lacandón custom of leaving handprints. They can help interpret the ceremonies shown in art. Physical anthropologists study bones and physical artifacts; they know how to determine the composition and the age of paint used in murals. Archaeologists uncover ruins, then study and preserve them. At Bonampak it was an archaeologist who knew that kerosene would help bring out the color of the murals without ruining them. These scientists worked together to interpret the Bonampak discoveries.

Never before had such details of Maya life been seen. Most Maya art uses symbols to depict gods and religious signs, but the murals of Bonampak are very realistic, showing scenes of daily life. One scientist called Bonampak "a pictorial encyclopedia." He said, "The city comes to life there again, with its ceremonies and processions."[6]

A New View of the Maya

The murals at Bonampak changed scholarly opinion about the Maya. For example, some historians previously had thought of the Maya as

9

Archaeologists work on an excavation. Using small shovels, they skim away soil a little at a time. The soil is then dumped into sieves and sifted for artifacts.

totally peaceful people. They had contrasted the peaceful Maya with the warrior Aztecs, a Mexican civilization which sacrificed human beings to the gods.

Why had historians and anthropologists thought that the Maya were peaceful? Partly because Maya sculpture does not show battle scenes. The murals at Bonampak, however, indicate that around A.D. 800, the Maya engaged in raids and surprise attacks. They also show that human sacrifice may have taken place.

The murals also changed beliefs about the role of women in Maya society. The murals show many women observing and even participating in ceremonies. Cultural anthropologists previously had thought that women played no role in Maya religious ceremonies. Why had they thought this? Anthropologists had observed that modern Lacandón women avoided religious sites. The anthropologists assumed that this also had occurred in classical Maya times. Now since the discovery of the Bonampak murals, many anthropologists think that women may once have enjoyed many rights in Maya civilization, but later lost them. Perhaps as the society paid more tribute to male warriors, it began to find women less valuable.[7]

A military spirit might have signaled the end of the Maya civilization. The Maya had flourished for about six hundred years. They had developed a calendar and a writing system. They created beautiful temples and sculptures. Did the Maya then suddenly begin to change? Did they start to think more about war and less about culture? We don't know for sure. But their civilization did begin to crumble around A.D. 850—only about fifty years after artists painted the battle scenes on the walls at Bonampak.

The ruins of Troy consist of nine layers dating back to prehistoric times.

II 2 II

BEAUTY AND CONFLICT IN TROY

Troy—the name recalls a city, a war, and a beauty contest. It was not an ordinary beauty contest, but a contest among goddesses. Hera, the jealous queen of Olympia; Athena, the goddess of wisdom; and Aphrodite, the goddess of love argued one day about their beauty. Who was the most beautiful? As they quibbled back and forth, they walked together down the slope of Mount Ida. Suddenly they came upon a shepherd, and they put their question to him: Who was the most beautiful? Each goddess tried to win favor with the shepherd: Hera offered power, Athena tempted him with wisdom, but Aphrodite offered the hapless shepherd the loveliest woman in the world to wed if he would pick Aphrodite herself as the most beautiful goddess. And so he did.

The shepherd was really no shepherd at all. He was Paris, son of Priam, the king of Troy. Soon he set sail on the Aegean Sea, seeking trade and adventure, and looking for the most beautiful woman in the world. He heard of a Greek woman in Sparta named Helen. Many said her beauty outshone that of any other woman. When Paris sailed to Sparta, he found Helen to be even more awesome than he had imagined. He fell hopelessly in love, and he brought Helen with him back to Troy.

All would have ended happily. However, a small detail stood in the way. Helen was already married. Her husband, King Menelaus, plotted revenge. Soon a thousand Greek warships headed toward Troy. Helen became known as "a face that launched a thousand ships."

Ancient Greeks told the story of Helen and Paris; a blind poet named Homer composed the *Iliad*. (Ilium was another name for Troy.) The *Iliad* tells of the terrible war that followed Paris's hasty act. It is impossible to know whether Helen and Paris existed, and no one believes any longer in the three goddesses. Many scholars do believe that Greece and Troy fought a long war. Three thousand years ago, both cities traded on the Aegean Sea, and both wanted control of the sea. Their economic rivalry may have led to war.

A Young Archaeologist

Scholars believe that the legend of Troy may be based in fact, partly because of the work of Heinrich Schliemann, an archaeologist who was born in Germany in 1822.

Troy sparked Henry Schliemann's imagination early in his life. From his father, he acquired a passion for ancient history. He visited German castles and listened to legends, and he believed in ghosts. He loved to hear stories about Troy. He refused to believe that the heroes had not really existed. And he was disappointed when his father told him that Troy had been completely destroyed.

In the book *Universal History for Children*, Schliemann found an engraving of Troy. The engraving showed the huge walls of the city in flames, with people running from the gates of the city to escape the fire. To the young Heinrich, this proved that Troy had not been completely destroyed. He called out: "Father, you were mistaken: [the artist] must have seen Troy. Otherwise, he couldn't have represented it here."

"My son, that is a mere fanciful picture," his father explained.

"If such walls once existed, they cannot possibly have been completely destroyed," young Heinrich insisted.[1]

Troy: The Excavation

Schliemann, who grew up to be an extremely successful businessman, decided to use his money to follow his dream and search for Troy. In 1868, he toured Greece for a few weeks, then he took off across the Aegean Sea toward Turkey.

First Schliemann investigated Burnarbashi, which was ten miles from the Aegean Sea. He imagined Troy as a gleaming city with white marble buildings and majestic gates, but at Burnarbashi, he found a rubbish heap. Homer had described Troy as being near the seashore, so Schliemann decided to investigate the site at Hissarlik.

Schliemann wanted to begin digging at the site, which included a hill and a plain below, like those described in the *Iliad*. His companions urged him not to be too hasty; it would be best to begin in the spring when the weather was better. Also, to dig he needed permission from the Turkish government.

The New Science of Archaeology

In the late 1800s, archaeology was a new science. For centuries, people had collected ancient artifacts for their own pleasure. Archaeologists, however, were interested in learning from artifacts. Artifacts are human-made objects that can be moved about without changing their appearance. (A vase is an artifact, for example, but a bridge is not.) Features are human-made objects that are difficult to move about. These would include bridges, campfire remains, and trash pits. In addition to features and artifacts, small bits of bone, shell, and charcoal help archaeologists to date and classify their finds.

Archaeologists started to think about the ethics of their profession. Today it would be considered unethical for an archaeologist to keep artifacts for profit. Archaeologists respect the rights of the countries where they work. They believe that artifacts should be used to help all people know about the past, so their finds usually are displayed in museums or are given to universities for study.

Schliemann wanted to be part of the new science of archaeology, but at the same time, he longed to find buried treasure for his own profit. He returned to Hissarlik in the spring of 1870 and began to dig. He found many artifacts: broken pieces of pottery, coins, lance-heads of green stone, and boars' tusks. These appeared to him to be very primitive, and they seemed to be older than the time of the Trojan War, which historians thought took place around 1200 B.C.

At first, Schliemann was not careful to record information

about his discoveries, but he listened eagerly to the advice of scientists, who told him that he must keep a journal. He must record the date and time of each discovery and the exact location where he unearthed each article. One scientist warned him, "You must take care to report these things accurately. Or else you will never be able to come to definite conclusions on your wonderful discoveries."[2]

German archaeologist Heinrich Schliemann discovered the ruins of Troy.

Heeding all of this advice, Schliemann became more scientific in his approach. He discovered that nine separate cities had been built at Hissarlik. Some were older than Troy, one perhaps from 3000 B.C. Some were more recent, the most recent possibly from 300 B.C. Schliemann, confident that one of the nine cities surely was the Troy of legends, named his findings according to legend. He named one immense wall after the goddess Athena; he named a statue of a woman after Helen of Troy.

Priam's Treasure

Early one morning in 1873, Schliemann dug up a broken chest with several silver vases inside it. Schliemann suspected that the chest held even more valuables, but he wanted to be careful. No one but his wife, Sophia, should know. If this were a treasure, then he would keep it for himself. "You must go at once and shout 'paidos'!" he whispered to Sophia.[3] (*Paidos* means "rest period" in Greek.) The workmen shuffled away from the site. They were grateful for some time off. Slowly, carefully, Heinrich and Sophia dug up the chest, wrapping its contents in Sophia's enormous red shawl. They sneaked away from the excavation site, ran to their house, and locked the door.

The Schliemanns spread out their treasure on a wooden table. Gold and silver sparkled. Red copper glowed. Goblets, vases, daggers, earrings, rings, and buttons dazzled their eyes. Most amazing of all was an elaborate headdress. Tassels hung from its sides. Many gold rings covered its forehead. When Heinrich placed the headdress on Sophia's head, he saw his wife turn into the beautiful Helen of Troy. He was sure he had found the glittering gold of his dreams. He called this find Priam's treasure.

Schliemann did not report his find to the government of Turkey. He smuggled the treasure out of Turkey and left Troy, returning for a while to Greece. Wanting praise and recognition from real archaeologists, he did not keep his find secret; he wrote about Priam's treasure and published photographs of all the beautiful artifacts. Furious Turkish government officials vowed never to allow Schliemann to return. Priam's treasure impressed some archaeologists, but others felt that Schliemann was no better than a pirate.

Failures and Successes

Eventually, Schliemann received permission to return to Troy, and he also excavated several sites in Greece, but he never was accepted or fully trusted by archaeologists. Schliemann had acted irresponsibly in running off with Priam's treasure, and he had made claims without enough evidence. For example, he had no real proof that the treasure he found had belonged to Priam. Schliemann's mistakes illustrate the value of careful and ethical work.

In spite of his rash behavior, Schliemann did contribute to the emerging science of archaeology. His many popular and colorful books about his adventures sparked an interest in Troy among ordinary people. The public supported and followed the work of archaeologists

According to legend, Greek soldiers hid in a large wooden horse in order to capture Troy. Today tourists can see a reproduction of the horse at the ruins of Troy in northwest Turkey.

who continued Schliemann's work. Scientists soon found more artifacts at Hissarlik. They dated and classified them. Some archaeologists today believe that one of the nine cities at Hissarlik truly is the legendary Troy.

The ruins of Machu Picchu lie in the striking terraced mountains of Peru.

⫼3⫼

TALL CITY OF SILENT STONE

"It fairly took my breath away. What could this place be? Why had no one given us any idea of it?"[1] With these words, Hiram Bingham remembered his first view of Machu Picchu, in 1911. For centuries the ancient city had been deserted. Hidden in a remote area of Peru, it had not attracted visitors. Bingham felt the city's loneliness and majesty. His journey there had been a trying one, but the splendor before his eyes made it worth the effort.

High in the Andes

The Inca had ruled in the Andes Mountains from about A.D. 1430 to A.D. 1532. Hiram Bingham had come to Peru hoping to find Inca ceremonial sites. A local farmer had encouraged Bingham to seek ruins on a mountain ridge called Machu Picchu. To get there, Bingham, who was not in good physical shape, first crossed rapids of a roaring river. A rickety bridge—some logs tied together with vines—offered the only way across. Bingham wrote, "No one could live for an instant in the icy cold rapids." They would "immediately be dashed to pieces against the rocks."[2] Bingham got down on his stomach to crawl slowly across the bridge, creeping along "six inches at a time."[3]

The most dangerous part of the journey lay ahead. Soon after he crossed the river, he found himself at the bottom of a steep slope. For over an hour he climbed, clawing the dirt with his fingernails. The heat and extreme humidity seemed more than he could bear. Several times he thought he would fall to his death, but finally he lifted himself up to the top of the slope.

He came upon a small hut where two farmers lived. They were descendants of highland Indians who had lived in the Inca empire. One of the farmers brought Bingham cool water in a drinking gourd. They allowed him to rest, gave him sweet potatoes to eat, and provided him with a young guide who would show him some ruins.

The guide led him to "beautifully constructed stone-faced terraces."[4] Bingham marveled at a curved temple and other structures. "Surprise followed surprise," he wrote. Most amazing was the stonework. With great artistic ability, the Incas had cut stones into fine geometrical shapes, each stone fitting perfectly together with another without any glue or mortar between them. Bingham could not even slip the slender blade of a knife through the stone fittings. The stones "might have grown together," Bingham wrote.[5]

The Inca were excellent engineers. They built roads and bridges through the steep and treacherous mountains. They used llamas as beasts of burden.

Figuring Out the Clues

Bingham wanted to identify the ruins, but jungle growth covered many of them. Bingham wrote that "massive trees, two feet thick, perched on the gable ends of small . . . houses."[6] He needed help. After a month or so, he left Machu Picchu. Within a year, he returned with workers who helped him chop away the jungle plants that hid the structures. The city that emerged amazed him. He tried to guess the use of each building; he wrote and spoke about his find. Soon other archaeologists arrived, and gradually a story about the Inca unfolded.

How can a deserted city tell a story? Think of a similar, modern example. Imagine that a family is far away from home. A stranger walks into their home and heads for a teenage boy's bedroom. The stranger wants to learn about the teenager by looking at his room. She notices that the bed is unmade. The clothes are strewn about. She looks at a CD collection and plays a few selections. She admires his aquarium and even feeds the fish. She finds some magazines and books under the bed. She writes their titles in a small notebook. She sketches the likeness of a poster she notices on the wall. She looks out the window and observes the bustling street below. Has the stranger learned anything about the teenager? Has the bedroom told a story?

A lost city cannot tell a complete story, but it can offer hints and clues, adding to a story that others have told. The Inca had no written language. Officials kept records with *quipa*, a system of counting that used knots on a cord. The knots are evidence of the Inca accounting system, but they do not tell us a lot about daily life. By looking at ruins, archaeologists can tell more about the Inca: They built roads, and they mastered stone architecture. They ruled an empire that extended north and south from Ecuador to Chile, stretching 2,500 miles. Such accomplishments require a lot of organization. Strong leaders must have exercised great power over lowly workers who carried the stones needed to build the temples and walls and roads.

When archaeologists investigated the ruins of Machu Picchu, they learned even more. They found many temples and shrines—more than had been found in most Inca cities. It seemed that Machu Picchu may have had special religious significance, as Bingham had thought. He liked to brag that Machu Picchu was the original, mythological home of Inca ancestors. Most archaeologists disagreed with him because none of the buildings showed evidence of the simple early Inca style. They thought that the Inca probably built the city in the 1500s, at the peak of their power. It was not their first home, but still it was probably a sacred place.

There are other clues today about the ancient Inca. Some of their descendants continue practicing what they say are old ways, and it is possible that some of their customs are similar to customs of the ancient Inca. For example, the descendants still live in the highland mountains, farming and weaving in a traditional manner.

Geography and climate are also helpful for understanding daily life in the past. Farming is difficult in high, rocky mountains. The stone terraces built by the Inca probably helped to level the land for farming.

It is also possible to learn about the Inca from their conquerors. The Inca were at the height of their power when the Spanish arrived in Peru in the 1500s. Some Spaniards recorded their impressions of the civilization. These writings help tell the story, but they must be read carefully, because they are not always fair or accurate. One Spanish historian of the 1500s described the Inca as "sheep without a shepherd."[7] In general, the Spaniards saw the Inca as enemies. They wanted Inca land and treasures, so their accounts were biased.

Inti-huatana   One mysterious structure at Machu Picchu baffled scientists. They eventually named the structure Inti-huatana. In the language of the Inca, this means "hitching post to the sun." (A hitching post is a place to tie up a riding animal.) The Inca did not ride horses; they used llamas and alpacas, which easily climb up steep mountains. The Inca sometimes tied them to hitching posts. But how could anyone tie up the sun?

The path to Inti-huatana passes a large chamber. Bingham guessed that the Incas displayed their dead in this chamber. He knew that explorers had found mummies in similar chambers in other parts of Peru. From Spanish writings, we know that the Inca mummified royal leaders when they died. They displayed them in rooms, and even carried them in parades, as a sign of respect to their lasting power. Spanish explorers named the chamber at Machu Picchu the Ornamental Chamber.

Above the Ornamental Chamber there are several terraces to climb. At the peak of a mountain ridge above the terraces is an impressive stone pinnacle, a point that rises six feet above a massive granite altar. One traveler wrote that the sun might appear

Inti-huatana, the hitching post to the sun.

to be tied up there for a moment. He said, "In his [the sun's] passage through his zenith, he might sit down in all his glory."[8]

This guess about the pinnacle made sense to archaeologists. It added to other information they had about the Inca's regard for the sun. One Spanish writer had noted that the Inca practiced astronomy, observing the movements of the sun in order to predict the best time to plant crops. "They calculated the month, day, hour and precise moment for sowing their crops."[9]

The Sun and Inca Religion

The sun also was important in the religion of the Inca. They worshiped the sun at a festival twice each year. A Spanish priest described this festival: The rulers dressed in magnificent robes; they wore headdresses of gold and silver. Awnings of beautiful feathers lined the avenues. As soon as the sunrise began, "they started to chant in marvelous harmony. . . . While chanting, each of them shook his foot."[10] As the sun rose, the chanting got louder and louder.

After the sunrise, young girls brought corn beer in pitchers. They also offered bales of coca to the sun. Everyone thanked the sun for past harvests, praying for future crops. As the day closed, the chanting began again, this time sounding to the Spanish priest like a sad murmur. As the sun sank in the sky, the voices died away.

The voices of Machu Picchu died away as well. After the Spaniards defeated the Inca in 1532, Inca civilization crumbled. No one knows for sure exactly when people deserted Machu Picchu or where they went. They probably settled in less remote areas in the mountains and farmed. Now shadows fall on the abandoned city, but so does the sun. For a moment each day it seems to stop, tied to a hitching post.

This citadel marks the site of Mohenjo-daro, believed to be one of the wealthiest and most prosperous Indus Valley cities.

4

CITIES OF THE INDUS VALLEY

"The attackers left the dead lying where they fell. In one of the houses sprawled thirteen skeletons—men, women, and children—some wearing bracelets, rings, and beads, and two of them with sword cuts on their skulls. . . . Elsewhere again, yet another skeleton was found in a lane. And all these grim relics lay on the highest and latest level of the city, witness to its last moments."[1]

Sir Mortimer Wheeler, a respected scholar of Indus civilization, described the gruesome scene. He was commenting on the end of a great city that flourished in the Indus Valley from 2500 B.C. to about 1500 B.C. This city, Mohenjo-daro, and its sister city, Harappa, first cradled civilization on the Indian subcontinent. The two cities had prospered for nearly a thousand years.

Commerce and river trade helped support the two cities, but they drew their greatest wealth from agriculture. Wheat, barley, dates, field peas, and even cotton prospered on the fertile soil of the Indus river valley. Mohenjo-daro lay near the Indus River in what today is Pakistan. Harappa lay about four hundred miles northeast on the Ravi River—a tributary of the mighty Indus.

Accomplished Artisans

The wealth from agriculture supported many crafts. Toolmakers crafted chisels, axes, knives, and other tools from bronze and copper. Potters used wheels to throw pots, and then painted them with red ochre. Weavers wove cotton into garments. Some artisans must have even known how to create statues using molds. Among the ruins, archaeologists found a statue of a pert and pretty dancer cast in bronze.

The inhabitants had had leisure time. They threw dice and played board games. They made toys for their children: little birds and tiny carts with wheels—miniatures of real oxcarts that adults

Many seals were found at Mohenjo-daro and Harappa. Archaeologists believe that the seals were used to show ownership.

used for plowing. The people of these river cities evidently had a strong sense of ownership: Archaeologists found hundreds of seals, used for marking belongings, and decorated with a sunken pattern of an animal—elephants, rhinoceroses, antelopes, crocodiles, even unicorns. Most impressively, though, inscriptions marked each seal. Perhaps the inscriptions were personal names. No one knows for sure, because no one has been able to decipher them. Nonetheless, the inscriptions show that the people of the Indus valley had developed writing. About 1500 B.C., Aryans invaded the Indian subcontinent, and everything started to change.

Fort Destroyers

Until the 1920s, no one in modern times knew about the people of Mohenjo-daro and Harappa. Both cities lay buried and forgotten. It was thought that the warrior Aryans were the first to bring civilization to the Indus Valley. The Aryans, it was thought, had found wandering tribes when they arrived. Yet some scholars wondered: In the Aryan saga *Rig-Veda*, there were references to forts. Indra, chief god of the Aryans, was called *Purmamdara*, which means "fort destroyer." One passage described Indra destroying ninety forts; in another passage, Indra "rends forts as age consumes a garment."[2] Scholars wondered whether this meant that the conquering Aryans had found a settled civilization, rather than a nomadic people.

Excavation

In the 1920s, the Indian Archaeological Survey excavated many sites in the Indus Valley. It was during these excavations that archaeologists unearthed the cities: first Harappa, and then Mohenjo-daro.

Harappa, a city about three miles in circumference, stood on a huge mound. Its most remarkable structure, a citadel about 460 yards long and 215 yards wide, rose high above the city. Bastions projected above the fort, a mighty baked-brick wall surrounded it, and gates prevented enemies from entering. To the north of the fort stood huge granaries. Straight streets ran in a perfect grid.

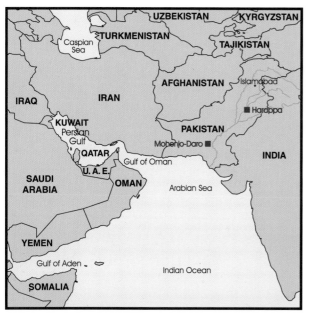

On the streets, modest but spacious houses once stood. They contained bathrooms and latrines. The city had excellent sewer and drainage systems.

Mohenjo-daro, just like its sister city, boasted a towering citadel and huge granaries. The plan of the city followed a design similar to that of Harappa. Sewers and drainage systems were evident. Most impressive was a huge public bath, made watertight with baked bricks. Archaeologists found these structures in even better condition than those at Harappa. The mystery of the forts mentioned in the *Rig-Veda* had evidently been solved.

A Lesson of Ecology

The skeletons described by Wheeler testify to many raids on the cities, but scholars do not hold the Aryans completely responsible for the decline of the ancient civilization. Many other factors may have caused its fall. Some anthropologists who specialize in environmental issues speculate that the ecology of the region may have been a factor. The rivers had been a source of wealth for the inhabitants, offering trade routes and soil fertile from flooding. But the rivers could also have contributed to problems.

Some theorize that the inhabitants may have destroyed the forests surrounding the rivers.[3] The Indus and Ravi valley people used huge quantities of baked bricks in their structures. Some anthropologists reason that the inhabitants kept cutting down trees for fuel to bake the bricks. For about a thousand years, structures continually had to be mended and rebuilt. Old cities crumbled, and new ones were built on top of them. As trees were cut down, the bare hills no longer absorbed the water from heavy rains. The rainwater could rush down the hills to the swelling river, and even high dikes might fail. As the people struggled with floods, their resources and energy may have dwindled. When Aryan invaders challenged them, the weakened inhabitants could not defend their magnificent forts.

This figurine, believed to portray a king, was excavated at Mohenjo-daro.

Mount Vesuvius looms above the ruins of Pompeii.

‖ 5 ‖

FROM THE ASHES OF VESUVIUS

Imagine a day, "blacker and denser than any ordinary night."[1] The earth trembles. The wind rocks the sea. Wild and dangerous waves slap the shore. On August 25, A.D. 79, doom sounded for Roman towns along the coast of the Bay of Naples. Many thought the world was coming to an end. People had lived for centuries under the shadow of a mountain called Vesuvius, but they had not realized that that mountain was really a volcano.

On August 24, a cloud of "unusual size and appearance" rose like a mushroom on a stem and then split off.[2] Ashes began to dust the land; blackened stones and bits of pumice fell from the sky. By nightfall, "broad sheets of fire and leaping flames" blazed on Mount Vesuvius.[3] Some of the citizens in the towns of Pompeii and Herculaneum prepared to flee; others fortified themselves in their homes.

Unfortunately, the worst was still to come. The next day, ash fell at the rate of six inches per hour, devouring the town of Pompeii. An avalanche surged through the town of Herculaneum; black winds raged. Those who had remained in their homes could no longer escape; they suffocated or were crushed as buildings toppled. Some were flung into the air by the powerful winds.

A Firsthand Account

An unusual document tells the tale of August in 79 A.D. Pliny the Younger wrote an eyewitness account of the volcano. He did not live in the shadow of the volcano, but he did live in a town across the bay. As the sky darkened, Pliny watched with his uncle, Pliny the Elder, who sailed off to investigate. The uncle never returned home; dense fumes choked and killed him as he reached the opposite shore.

Pliny the Younger described the events of that August with chilling detail in an account that has survived for nearly two thousand years. After Pliny's time, everyone assumed that the two towns had been totally destroyed.

Discovery

In 1709, a laborer was digging a shaft in the Italian town of Ercolano, near Naples, when his shovel struck a layer of ancient white marble. The white marble turned out to be part of a Roman theater. Ercolano, as it happened, had been built on Herculaneum, and the theater had been buried for almost two thousand years. Word of the discovery spread, but it was only in 1748 that some other workmen digging by a canal found remains of Herculaneum's sister city. This time the workers struck upon bronze and marble statues, and an inscription marking the site as ancient Pompeii.

Unfortunately, the rulers of Naples, who did not care very much about history, looted the theater, carting off slabs of marble and bronze statues. They even forced prisoners to dig tunnels to find more treasure. At this time, the science of archaeology did not exist; there was no code of ethics to stop the plunderers.

However, noxious gases beneath the ground slowed the looters down. Also, because the Italian government did not want to destroy Ercolano, it did not have the entire site dug up. Nonetheless, for over one hundred years, scavengers took valuable art, stones, and gems.

This photograph shows the ruins of an elegant estate, the House of the Faun, in Pompeii.

A Serious Excavation

By 1860, when archaeology had become a recognized science, archaeologists began excavations of Herculaneum and Pompeii. They soon found that the volcano had buried the towns without completely destroying them. Some of the mud from the volcano was extremely hot, carbonizing whatever it touched. Some of the mud was warm, preserving delicate items; even some of the food had not rotted away after two thousand years. Excavators found fruit in glass containers in the market, and carbonized loaves of bread in a bakery shop oven. They also easily identified the skeletons of fish and sheep in a butcher shop. In one house, excavators found a table set for dinner. In the corner stood a pitcher for hot water and a brazier for cooking. On the wall, a sign warned about proper manners: "Don't put your dirty feet on our couch covers. If you bicker at the table, you'll have to go home. Be modest and don't make eyes at another man's wife."[4]

Amusing signs and graffiti could be found throughout the towns. Love complaints were scribbled on

Many of Pompeii's buildings were found in the same condition their frightened owners had left them. These storage jars, called amphorae, were found in a shop.

walls along with bawdy jokes. There were signs advertising the price of wine, rent rates, and rewards for stolen property. Archaeologists found election slogans painted in red and black on many shop walls. Each trade—fishermen, dyers, bakers, and goldsmiths—urged citizens to vote for its candidate for mayor; one painted slogan even advertised the preferred candidate of street thieves![5]

This was a valuable find. In 1860, no one really knew what life in ancient Rome had been like. Although there were stone ruins throughout Europe, they showed only a small part of Roman life. These buried towns filled in many details. For example, the numerous election slogans testified to the strength of democracy in ancient Rome; graffiti suggested widespread literacy. One joker scribbled on a wall, "Everybody writes on the walls but me."[6] The ruins also revealed something about social class in ancient Rome. Fine jewelry, paintings, and statues revealed one side of life; taverns and obscene drawings showed another.

A Tragedy Uncovered

Even today, parts of ancient Pompeii and Herculaneum remain buried. In 1982, scientists unearthed the scene of a heartbreaking tragedy in Herculaneum. The never before seen skeletons lay in beach chambers, dressing rooms near the ocean. In one chamber, a family huddled together. A baby lay cradled in the arms of an adult. Another skeleton lay with its face to the ground, perhaps crying into a pillow.[7]

From these skeletons, scientists have learned something about the volcano. The position and location of the skeletons suggest that these people met sudden death, that the hot mud and gas from the volcano rushed down the mountain at great speed. Scientists have observed such an event, called a glowing avalanche, after certain other volcanic eruptions. The skeletons showed that a glowing avalanche probably had occurred at Herculaneum.

Sara Bisel, a physical anthropologist, examined the skeletons for even more information. "Who says dead men don't talk?" Dr. Bisel exclaimed when she first saw the skeletons. "These bones will have a lot to say."[8]

Dr. Bisel gave each of the skeletons a name. One of her favorites was Pretty Lady, who had small, sturdy bones and a well-proportioned face. Her nose was slender and her teeth were in perfect condition. In general, Dr. Bisel found very few cavities among the skeletons, which suggested that their diet included very little sugar. In spite of Pretty Lady's beauty, she was not a lady of leisure. Dr. Bisel could tell by the shape of her bones that she had strong arm muscles and that she worked hard. Dr. Bisel guessed that she had been a weaver.

Each skeleton had a story: One person lived the hard life of a slave; another had scars from battles. One wore expensive rings and bracelets. One died carrying her first child in her womb. Sara Bisel proved her point: Dead men, and dead women, could speak from the ashes of Vesuvius.

Chapter 1

1. Karl Ruppert, "Location, Environment, and History of the Site" in Karl Ruppert, J. Eric S. Thompson, and Tatiana Proskouriakoff, *Bonampak, Chiapas, Mexico* (Washington D.C.: Carnegie Institution, 1955), p. 8.

2. Ibid.

3. Andre Emmerich, *Art Before Columbus* (New York: Simon and Schuster, 1963), p. 139.

4. J. Eric S. Thompson, "The Subject Matter of the Murals" in Ruppert, Thompson, and Proskouriakoff, p. 53.

5. Ibid. p. 56.

6. Jacques Soustelle quoted in Charles Gallenkamp, *The Riddle and Rediscovery of a Lost Civilization* (New York: David McKay Company, 1976) p. 151.

7. J. Eric S. Thompson, "Some Ethnological Notes on the Murals" in Ruppert, Thompson, and Proskouriakoff, p. 64.

Chapter 2

1. This quotation is reported by Schliemann in his autobiography and reproduced in Leo Deuel, *Memoirs of Heinrich Schliemann: A Documentary Portrait Drawn from His Autobiographical Writings, Letters, and Excavation Reports* (New York: Harper & Row, 1977), p. 25.

2. Robert Payne, *The Gold of Troy* (New York: Funk & Wagnalls, 1959), p. 155.

3. Ibid., p. 164.

Chapter 3

1. Hiram Bingham, *Lost City of the Incas* (New York: Atheneum, 1979), p. 153.

2. Ibid., p. 149.

3. Ibid., p. 149.

4. Ibid., p. 151.

5. Ibid., p. 153.

6. Quoted in John Hemming, *Machu Picchu* (New York: Newsweek, 1981), p. 18.

7. Garcilasco de la Vega, *Royal Commentaries of the Incas, Part One* (Austin: University of Texas Press, 1966), p. 31.

8. George Squier, quoted in Hemming, p. 50.

9. Quoted in Hemming, p. 51.

10. Ibid.

Chapter 4

1. Sir Mortimer Wheeler, "The Civilization of a Sub-Continent," *The Dawn of Civilization*, ed. Stuart Piggott (New York: McGraw-Hill Book Company, 1961), p. 249.

2. Rig-Veda quoted in *The Horizon Book of Lost Worlds*, ed. Marshall B. Davidson (New York: American Heritage Publishing Company, 1962), p. 210.

3. See Bridget Allchin and Raymond Allchin, *The Rise of Civilization in India and Pakistan* (Cambridge: Cambridge University Press, 1982), pp. 224–225, and Davidson, p. 218, for a discussion of ecological issues.

Chapter 5

1. Pliny the Younger is excerpted in Michael Grant, *Cities of Vesuvius* (New York: Penguin, 1978), pp. 28–30.

2. Ibid.

3. Ibid.

4. Paul MacKendrick, *Mute Stones Speak* (New York: W.W. Norton, 1983), p. 254.

5. Ibid., p. 249.

6. Helen H. Tanzer, *The Common People of Pompeii: A Study of the Graffiti* (Baltimore: Johns Hopkins University Press, 1939), p. 6.

7. Rick Gore, "The Dead Do Tell Tales at Vesuvius," *National Geographic* (May 1984), pp. 557–614.

8. Ibid.

A.D.—A way to refer to the time after what is thought to be the birth year of Jesus Christ. The letters stand for the Latin words *anno Domini*. The year 2000 will be two thousand years after the time of Jesus Christ.

anthropology—The study of human beings, their origins and culture.

archaeology—The study of the remains of past human cultures.

artifact—A simple object showing human workmanship. An artifact can be moved without being harmed or changed.

Asia Minor—A peninsula in the western part of Asia. Most of modern Turkey lies in Asia Minor.

astronomy—The study of heavenly bodies, such as stars and planets.

B.C.—A way to refer to the time before what is thought to be the birth year of Jesus Christ. The letters stand for "before Christ."

Glossary

carbonization—The process of turning to charcoal.

descendants—People who come from common ancestors. For example, some modern Indians of southern Mexico are descendants of the Maya.

ecology—The study of the systems in nature and how they relate to one another.

engraving—Artwork made by cutting figures into wood or other material.

ethics—A system of moral behavior.

excavation—The digging up of something; for example, an ancient civilization.

feature—A large, complex object showing human workmanship. A feature cannot be moved without being harmed or changed.

fortify—To make strong.

glowing avalanche—An avalanche is a large mass of material, such as snow or rocks, that speeds down a mountain. A glowing avalanche is made of superhot gas and debris.

inscription—Something written, for example, on a monument.

mural—Wall painting.

nomads—A member of a wandering people who have no permanent home.

physical anthropology—The study of human physical characteristics, such as bones.

pinnacle—The high point of a building or mountain.

pumice—A glass rock naturally produced during volcanic eruptions.

Roman Empire—The kingdom of ancient Rome that included parts of what are now Europe, Asia, and Africa. The empire existed from about 300 B.C. to A.D. 476.

temple—A building used for religious practice.

terrace—A raised area, made for a road or planting, with the top leveled flat.

Trojan Horse—Part of the legend of the Trojan War. According to legend, Greek soldiers hid in a wooden horse that the Trojans brought inside the Troy city gates. During the night, the Greeks crept out of the horse and opened the gates, letting all the other Greek soldiers into the city. The war ended when the Greeks set Troy afire.

Trojan War—According to legend, a ten-year war around 1200 B.C. in which Greece conquered Troy.

volcano—A vent in the earth from which hot lava, and melted rock, and ash come out, sometimes explosively.

zenith—The highest point of a heavenly journey. When the moon is farthest from the earth, it is at its zenith.

400,000 B.C.—Oldest evidence of human shelters.

25,000 B.C.—Cave paintings in Lascaux, France and Altamira, Spain.

8,000 B.C.—The first cities appeared in Mesopotamia (modern Iraq) and Anatolia (modern Turkey).

3000 B.C.—Old Kingdom of Egypt rises. Settlement of Troy. The Indus Valley Civilization arises.

2700 B.C.—The first pyramids are built in Egypt.

2500 B.C.—The Indus Valley Civilization begins to flourish.

1500 B.C.—The Indus Valley Civilization is destroyed by Aryan invaders.

1200 B.C.—Destruction of Troy. Remains show city was destroyed by fire and abandoned for four hundred years.

900-700 B.C.—Time during which Homer lived and composed the *Iliad*.

800 B.C.—First settlement of Pompeii by Oscans, an ancient people of Italy.

753 B.C.—The legendary date of the founding of Rome.

B.C.
A.D.

300 B.C.—Pompeii is conquered by Rome.

A List of Important Dates

79—Mount Vesuvius erupts and destroys the Roman cities of Pompeii, Herculaneum, and Stabiae.

c. **250**—Classic Maya civilization begins.

c. **800**—The Walls of Bonampak are painted by Mayan artisans.

c. **850**—Bonampak is abandoned.

c. **900**—End of Classic Maya civilization.

1100-1200—Inca civilization begins.

1492—Columbus lands in the New World.

1532—Incas conquered by Spanish.

1748—Pompeii is rediscovered.

1870—Heinrich Schliemann begins excavations at Hissarlik, Turkey.

1911—Machu Picchu discovered by Hiram Bingham.

1922—Rediscovery of Mohenjo-Daro.

1946—The Lacandón show the painted walls of Bonampak to Giles Healy.

Beck, Barbara L. *The Incas*. Revised by Lorna Greenberg. New York: Franklin Watts, 1983.

Blassingame, Wyatt. *The Incas and the Spanish Conquistadores*. New York: Julian Messner, 1980.

Burrell, Roy. *The Greeks*. Illustrated by Peter Connolly. Oxford, England: Oxford University Press, 1990.

Casson, Lionel. *Daily Life in Ancient Rome*. New York: McGraw-Hill Book Company, 1975.

Davidson, Marshall D., ed. *The Horizon Book of Lost Worlds*. New York: American Heritage Publishing Company, 1962.

Gore, Rick. "The Dead Do Tell Tales at Vesuvius." *National Geographic* (May 1984), pp. 557–614.

Lattimore, Deborah Nourse. *Why There Is No Arguing in Heaven: A Mayan Myth*. New York: Harper and Row, 1989.

Meyer, Carolyn, and Charles Gallenkamp. *The Mystery of the Ancient Maya*. New York: Atheneum, 1985.

Ventura, Piero, and Gian P. Ceserani. *In Search of Troy*. Englewood Cliffs, N.J.: Silver Burdett, 1985.

Watson, Jane Werner. *The Iliad and The Odyssey*. Adapted from Homer. New York: Golden Press, 1964.

Index